MAKING
YOUR MARK

MAKING YOUR MARK

*How to Develop a Personal
Marketing Plan for Becoming More
Visible and More Appreciated at Work*

Deborah Shouse

SkillPath Publications
Mission, Kansas

Project Editor: Kelly Scanlon

Editor: Jane Doyle Guthrie

Cover and Book Design: Rod Hankins

Library of Congress Catalog Card Number: 95-69805

ISBN: 1-878542-98-2

10   9   8   7   6   5   4   99

Printed in the United States of America

Contents

V

On Your Mark

"How many of you work for large corporations?" the speaker asks a business networking club.

In the room of seventy people, one person raises her hand.

"How many of you used to work for large corporations?"

Twenty-five people raise their hands.

You've probably seen a lot of people stuck in their company slot or by-passed when promotions come along. You've seen people who work hard and are never rewarded.

2

You've probably also seen many of your co-workers and friends "right-sized" into different companies, sometimes even into different careers.

Every day you read about some major business change: from downsizing to transferring, from mergers to bankruptcy.

In today's business world, it's not enough to do your work well. You need to be perceived as a valuable and outstanding contributor to your company.

Raising your visibility and increasing your perceived value at work—that's what *Making Your Mark* helps to accomplish. This book is a mini-seminar in marketing your most valuable asset—yourself!

You're already working hard and doing outstanding things, so you might as well get recognition and credit for them.

You can read this book in small bites of time, or work through it in one full-course sitting. The marketing plan you create will help you, regardless of your industry, business size, or job tittle.

Developing your marketing plan gives you a focus for your energies. By simply creating this plan, you'll broaden your business network and become more knowledgeable about your company.

Each chapter helps you to focus on and develop one aspect of your plan.

Chapter 1, "Attention Shoppers: Why Market Yourself," explains the importance of having a personal marketing plan. Your personal marketing campaign lets your boss know the good news about you and your accomplishments. You, your boss, and your department and company benefit from your self-marketing expertise.

Chapter 2, "Target Audience: Defining the Bull's Eye," helps you identify the people who can help you become successful. Managers, directors, co-workers, secretaries—these are some of the people who will make your marketing plan successful. But before you explore the people behind your success, explore the persona of your company itself. For your marketing strategy, delve into the emotional underpinnings of your company.

In Chapter 3, "Product Profile: The Good News About You," you will explore some of the qualities and characteristics that you want to project. Every person—including you—has a unique niche. An important step in your self-marketing plan is defining the qualities you want to project. Think of yourself as a new product facing a competitive marketplace. Use these product-oriented marketing concepts when you create your product profile.

In Chapter 4, "Power Partners: You Don't Have to Do This Alone," you find out how to bring together the people who can help you build your marketing plan. Form a lunch group and brainstorm ways to increase your recognition. Seek a marketing mentor who can guide and advise you.

Chapter 5, "Positioning Poses: Creating the Perception," helps you define your public persona. Your magic is real. To prepare your audience to believe how great you are, you need to create the proper image and then drum up the demand. Decide on the image you want to project—competent? thoughtful? get it done?—and then create your positioning prowess.

Finally, Chapter 6, "Power Plan: Implementing Your Marketing Strategies," shows you how to put your plan into action. How often do scenes of success drift into your mind? You'd like more money, more prestige, more visibility, more recognition, more responsibility... Whatever "more" motivates you, now is the time to push beyond the wishful thinking stage and make it happen. With your calendar, begin building the marketing strategies you've created.

So...On Your Mark...Get Set...Go "Make Your Mark."

Attention Shoppers:

Why Market Yourself?

You've just finished a huge project within budget and two days early. You put the report on your boss's desk and wait for her to heap praise on you.

Days go by. No heap of praise. No little mound of praise. Not even an encouraging nod.

Finally your boss appears and, with an apologetic smile, says: "Here's another project for you. I need it by next Wednesday."

6 Is she crazy, insensitive, or just totally swamped with her own work and thus unaware of your recent great accomplishment?

Help-Yourself Marketing

A personal marketing campaign lets your boss know the good news about you and your accomplishments. You, your boss, your department, and your company benefit from your self-marketing expertise. When you develop a personal marketing plan, you:

- Go from "shelf to self" in your boss's eyes.
- Double your visibility and value.
- Get the recognition you deserve.
- Understand your company.
- Model communications for others.
- Put your job to work for you.

To visualize going from "shelf to self," imagine the detergent section of a grocery store. Rows of good-looking boxes holding similar types of products. How do you know which box holds the most effective ingredients? How you do know which detergent is reliable? Which is long-lasting and guaranteed for results? The detergent companies aren't too shy about making their products visible and telling you how unique each one is.

When you market *yourself,* you gain visibility throughout your company and possibly within the industry and community. You take your *self* "off the shelf" and show people who you are and how you contribute uniquely to the overall effort.

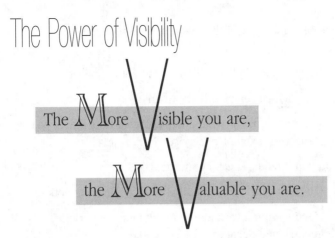

The More Visible you are,

the More Valuable you are.

That's the "Double MV Theory" of personal marketing. Being visible means letting people know your strengths and how you help the company and community. Are you creative outside the workplace? Do you volunteer? Are you involved in special workplace projects?

Your visibility enhances your department, your co-workers, and your boss. Next time a special project comes up, you may be considered for the planning committee.

Are you making the most of your visibility power? Consider the following situations to find out:

1. You win an award for sports. You:

   A. Whisper it to your best friend at a lunch break.

   B. Kick a ball around the lunchroom and hope someone notices.

   C. Make copies of your picture receiving the award and send it to your company newsletter.

2. You have consistently finished each project on time and within budget for the last year. You:

   A. Hope you'll receive a nice bonus.

   B. Tell a few friends you're hoping for a bonus.

   C. Write down a list of your accomplishments on a single sheet of paper and present it to your boss.

3. You brought in six of the seven new customers for the quarter. You:

   A. Look in the mirror and wonder how it happened.

   B. Call each customer and say "thank you."

   C. Ask a customer to write a letter to your department head about your exemplary service.

4. You win a public-speaking award. You:

   A. Put the award on your wall and hope someone notices it.

   B. Mention your award loudly in the lunchroom during an impassioned debate with a co-worker.

   C. Send a memo on the award to the director of human resources and offer to give a lunch-time workshop on presentation skills.

5. You recently were elected an officer in a local professional group. You:

   A. Wear your name tag from the group to work.

   B. Invite a co-worker to attend a meeting with you.

   C. Create a press release and let your boss, as well as the local newspapers, know of this honor.

If you answered all C's, you're already "C-ing" your name in lights. B's mean you're in the people-to-people stage, passing the information shyly. Too many A's mean you need to learn to crow!

The peacock can't afford to let its tail drag in the dust. Yes, it's a pretty bird, but so is the canary, the cardinal, and the blue jay. But when the peacock displays its unique, vibrant feathers, everyone becomes transfixed.

No one will guess how great you are, and few will pause to ask about your accomplishments, unless you display your skills. Make it easy for people to understand what a great tale you have to tell. Without being egoistic or aggressive, give people the information they need to understand your excellence.

Your personal marketing plan will get you the recognition you deserve. Marketing yourself means spreading the array of your talents so people understand you are G-R-E-A-T:

Gather—You know how to connect and to bring together the right people and resources.

roles—Your flexibility lets you play many roles in the company.

ethics—You have a positive attitude about work, you're loyal and contribute to the company.

abilities—You offer an array of job-related expertise, plus a variety of abilities outside work.

team—You are willing to work as a partner and share the glory.

10

Showing your GREATness gives people a way to praise you easily. Here's an example: Gary is rushing to a staff meeting. He's been in meetings all day and he's giving a speech this evening. He's busy and harried. Yet he stops you to say, "I really liked that article about your satisfied customer survey in the employee newsletter. I had an experience like that once and..."

When you share personal and business information, you give people a chance to connect with you and cheer you on. Be ready for the "applause" and accept it—graciously. Get out of the habit of always answering "Oh, that was a nothing," or "I can't take credit. Everyone helped me get done on time." Make your praisers feel good about sharing their enthusiasm. Enjoy your achievements and don't "shy" away from them. You have a right to really savor your accomplishments and to share your techniques with others.

By sharing your achievements, you're modeling a communication style that allows as much time for good news as bad.

The Company You Keep

The more you are aware of your unique market potential, the greater your opportunities. Developing your marketing plan sweeps you outside the narrow cubicle of your department and into the wide arena of your company.

The first step in creating your plan is learning who's who and what's what within the company. How do the marketing and fulfillment area work together? How does your company rank with the competition? What accomplishments is your company known for? How does your department contribute? How does your department affect the other departments? How does your work affect company image? The more you know, the more ways you can contribute, the more opportunities you can catch.

Ruth says, "Ever since I started contributing to the newsletter, things have been happening. My new goal is to meet one new person a week. This week, I'm having lunch with someone in the fulfillment department. I'm going to find out exactly what goes on there. I'm going to say, 'Is your work really *fulfilling?*'"

Make things happen with your new market-oriented attitude.

12 Making Your Mark Plus: The Sum of Things

You've just learned the benefits of your personal marketing plan. Sure, this plan is going to take thought, time, and work. But the benefits are worth it.

When you develop a personal marketing plan, you:

- Go from shelf to self in your boss's eyes.
- Double your visibility and value.
- Get the recognition you deserve.
- Understand your company.
- Model communications for others.
- Put your job to work for you.

Are you making the most of your visibility power?

List three recent accomplishments or activities you'd like to share with your boss, co-workers, and/or department:

1. _____

   _____

   _____

2. _____

   _____

   _____

3. _____

   _____

   _____

How to make them recognize your greatness? The first step to a successful marketing plan is analyzing your audience. Read on to find out how.

2

Target Audience:

Defining the Bull's Eye

- Your manager has three children and a full-time nanny to help her care for them. She has just finished an M.B.A., reads the stock market page every day, and subscribes to three financial periodicals. She likes to see the numbers on everything.

- The director of your division has a Ph.D. in education from an Ivy League school. Before she entered the corporate world, she worked for two years with the Peace Corps. She is a community activist and intensely people-oriented. She never makes a decision without consulting at least five others.

- Your co-worker Karl is single and loves race cars and the triathlon. He's fast on everything he does and mostly accurate. Competition really perks him up. He feels uneasy when he's stuffed into a team setting.

- Your assistant is retired from the military. He likes order and consistency. He likes to know your schedule in advance and resists making changes. In his spare time, he creates wonderful detailed dollhouses for his granddaughters and the children of friends.

These four very different people have two things in common: They work for the same company and they're part of your target audience. These are some of the people—management and co-workers—who will make your marketing plan successful. But before you explore the people behind your success, explore the persona of your company itself.

Zeroing in on Your Company

Is your company a big amorphous business with hundreds of employees or a small entrepreneurial venture with a core staff of twelve. Each company has its own culture and its own personality. Yours has a mission and possibly a vision that hopes to unite its people.

But that mission is just the beginning. For your marketing strategy, delve into the emotional underpinnings of your company. Look for the inner story that will help you answer, What does my company really want?

"Our company rewards employees who have an 'I'll do it no matter what attitude,'" says Charlotte, a CPA who works for a Big Eight firm. "Our company wants aggressive people who are always ready and pushing to do more."

"We seek quiet, low-key people who do their jobs well and without prodding," says Helen, a manager in a health care organization. "Our company rewards people who don't make a fuss, who do their work along with anything else they see needs doing. People who want to make changes cause stress here."

"We like people with ideas—and lots of them," says Kevin, who heads a small advertising agency.

"Team spirit is vital to our operation," says Tim, the director of a not-for-profit agency. "We value those who understand the art of compromise. We appreciate people who work for the greater good of the group."

Your goal is to increase your visibility and value and to gain recognition. Using information and intuition to decipher what your company values, you can create a corporate "persona" and show yourself the inside story—the foundation of your personal marketing plan.

To give yourself the building blocks of a strategy, complete the "Interview With Your Company" exercise on page 16. Spend some real thought on item 8 in the exercise, where you assimilate what you've learned and then describe the essence of your company. This profile provides a valuable way to focus your efforts when you create your personal marketing plan.

16 Interview With Your Company

Use your intuition on some of these questions. This is about impressions rather than facts.

1. Imagine your company as a person. Describe that person:

   ☐ Male   Age_____
   ☐ Female   Height_____ Weight_____

2. Education:

   ☐ High school   ☐ Undergrad
   ☐ Master's   ☐ Ph.D.
   ☐ Technical training   ☐ Other_____

3. Style of dress:

   ☐ Casual   ☐ Corporate
   ☐ Trendy   ☐ Artistic
   ☐ Other_____

4. How does the voice sound?

   ☐ Modulated   ☐ Soft
   ☐ Precise   ☐ Booming
   ☐ Deep   ☐ Other_____

5. What type of energy does your company have?

   ☐ Slow and deliberate   ☐ Fast-paced, impatient
   ☐ Moderate   ☐ Other_____

6. What about personality type? (check all that apply)

   ☐ People-oriented   ☐ Bottom-line oriented
   ☐ Wants to be the best in the market
   ☐ Detail-oriented

7. What animal does your company remind you of?

   _____

   _____

8. What color, and why?

_____

_____

9. Imagine you are sitting at a power lunch with your company. Ask it these questions:

What is your company concerned about? _____

_____

_____

What does it feel really proud of? _____

_____

_____

What does your company wish people knew about it? _____

_____

_____

What is its vision for the future? _____

_____

_____

_____

10. Now take what you've learned and write a paragraph that describes the essence of your company. Here's an example:

"The Write Stuff is a forward-thinking, people-oriented woman, dressed in purple and soaring like an eagle. The Write Stuff is proud of the quality and variety of her work, concerned that not enough people know about it. She loves change. She wishes more people knew about her teaching and creative writing capabilities. Her vision for the future is meaningful work that makes a difference for people and for the world."

18   Lining Up Your Target Market

You've seen the pages of demographics and statistics put together just to sell a single product. Understanding your audience (co-workers, managers, customers, etc.) is key to your marketing plan. Who are they and what do they want? How can you help them?

Beverly's been traveling around the country with her singing and comedy act. Last week she was in Vegas; this week, Branson, Missouri.

"You'll have to change some parts of the show for the Branson audience," her publicist cautions her.

"A song and joke are a song and joke, no matter where you are," Beverly says.

But the Branson audience has a different sense of humor than the one in Las Vegas. Only by knowing her audience can Beverly receive the applause she wants (to say nothing of filling the house and making a good living).

So who are these people who will "buy" your personal marketing message?

Consider a two-tiered approach to analyzing your audience. You're marketing yourself both to people of higher positions and to those of equal and lower ones. Buy-in by both tiers is crucial to your well-run marketing campaign:

Step 1. Create a profile of upper-level managers.

Step 2. Create a profile of your peers and support staff.

The tools for doing this lie in the "What's What About Who's Who" profile sheets on pages 20 to 23.* Just filling them out helps you focus and think about your audience, and then you can use the information in your marketing strategy.

---

* You may be able to get statistics from your Human Resources department. If not, use your intuition. Make educated guesses.

Here's an example of the descriptions you'll come up with:

Upper management is a college-educated group with postgraduate degrees, equally divided between men and women. They want more job security and more money. Personal goals include more time off, more leisure time, and more travel. They wish they had more support staff and more control over the vendors they use. They'd love to have a new office building with lots of new equipment and a fancy corporate dining room. They like down-to-earth memos.

My co-workers and support staff are 70 percent women, mostly college educated. They want more money and work that better uses their skills. Their personal goals include more time with their families. They like one-on-one communications.

What's What About Who's Who:

Profile of Your Managers, Directors, and Executives

1. Gender: M _____   F _____ (percentage of each)

2. List the positions above yours in the company as well as the numbers of employees in each.

   _____

   _____

   _____

   _____

   _____

   _____

3. Education (percentage of each):

   High school ____ Undergrad ____ Master's ____ Ph.D. ____

   Advanced technical training ____ Other_____

4. What are the three most common business goals of this group? (a promotion, a raise, a position that better uses personal skills, etc.)

   A. _____

   B. _____

   C. _____

5. What are the three most common personal goals of this group? (spend more time with the family, etc.)

   A. _____

   B. _____

   C. _____

6. What business challenges does this group face? (not enough time, not enough support staff, not enough clients, etc.)

A. _____

B. _____

C. _____

7. What does your audience wish for? (more time, money, education, information, silence, etc.)

A. _____

B. _____

C. _____

D. _____

8. How does your audience like to be communicated to?

☐ In writing   ☐ By telephone

☐ Electronically   ☐ In person ____

9. Compose a description of this audience, using as many of the above attributes as possible.

_____

_____

_____

_____

_____

_____

_____

_____

_____

_____

What's What About Who's Who:

Profile of Your Co-workers and Support Staff

1. Gender: M _____   F _____ (percentage of each)

2. List the positions equal to yours and supportive of yours in the company, as well as the number of employees in each.

_____

_____

_____

_____

_____

_____

_____

_____

3. Education (percentage of each):

   High school ____ Undergrad ____ Master's ____ Ph.D. ____

   Advanced technical training ____ Other_____

4. What are the three most common business goals of this group? (a promotion, a raise, a position that better uses personal skills, etc.)

   A._____

   B._____

   C._____

5. What are the three most common personal goals of this group? (spend more time with the family, etc.)

   A._____

   B._____

   C._____

6. What business challenges does this group face? (not enough time, not enough support staff, not enough clients, etc.)

A. _____

B. _____

C. _____

7. What does your audience wish for? (more time, money, education, information, silence, etc.)

A. _____

B. _____

C. _____

D. _____

8. How does your audience like to be communicated to?

☐ In writing ☐ By telephone

☐ Electronically ☐ In person ____

9. Compose a description of this audience, using as many of the above attributes as possible.

_____

_____

_____

_____

_____

_____

_____

_____

_____

_____

_____

- Joanne is a highly motivated support staff member. She's always ahead of things, anticipating what people need. One day when you're in the break room with Joanne, she mentions her dream of starting a non-profit agency to provide support for single mothers.

  "Everyone needs support," she says. You suddenly notice the creases around her eyes and the tremble in her lip. "I'd like my job to be helping other women get the assistance they need."

  You've just glimpsed another dimension of Joanne and caught sight of what motivates her.

- George often arrives at meetings late. He's easily distracted and frequently offers irrelevant remarks. One morning George walks into your office and closes the door.

  "Can you edit this for me?" he asks, a note of panic in his voice. "This proposal is due tomorrow and my secretary is out of town for a week."

  "Why don't you use the typing pool?" you ask.

  "My grammar and spelling are terrible," George says. "I'm the only one in my department without a college degree. I'm going to school three nights a week, but grammar is still hard for me."

  "I'll be happy to edit the proposal for you," you say. You now have a new insight into George's behavior.

One definition of marketing is figuring out what people want and getting it for them. Because you are an insider in your company, your marketing plan has an advantage: You have the insight and the foresight to understand the emotional context of your audience. What is motivating them, fueling their actions? What do they really want? Although Joanne's personal goals lie outside of work, they impact her performance. George's educational "secret" causes him worry, embarrassment, and extra stress.

If you interviewed the people in your company, many of them would reveal that work is not the number one priority issue in their lives. Be on the alert for the emotional subtext or undercurrent in your audience. Notice who volunteers for what, who's married with children, who's a single parent, who's going to college at night, who's working on a big outside project. Or better yet, fill out the "Emotion Detector" on page 26. This information can help you target your audience more meaningfully.

Going beyond the "facts" and into the feelings is one way to make your marketing strategy stick in people's minds. People remember those who connected with them in some emotional way.

Emotion Detector

Check off all answers that apply to your company's "emotional" side.

1. Types of community involvement your company encourages:

☐ Environmental   ☐ Political
☐ Social reform   ☐ Health-related
☐ Educational   ☐ Personal improvement
☐ Other_____

2. What types of groups do people in your company volunteer to help?

☐ Environmental   ☐ Political
☐ Social reform   ☐ Health-related
☐ Educational   ☐ Personal improvement
☐ Other_____

3. What populations does your company target or tend to work with?

☐ Infants/children ☐ Teens/ adults
☐ Seniors   ☐ People with disabilities
☐ People new to this country
☐ Other_____

4. How do people in your company spread the word when they want to raise money or share information about a cause they believe in?

☐ Memo   ☐ Word of mouth
☐ Direct mail to home ☐ Telephone
☐ Other_____

5. What kinds of notes are on the company bulletin board—
   things people ask for help with or things they're selling?

   _____

   _____

   _____

6. What are the main concerns you hear about through the
   company grapevine?

   _____

   _____

   _____

   _____

7. Now you have a bundle of emotions. Write a paragraph
   describing the emotional issues (concern about youth,
   environmental issues, etc.) for the people in your company.

   _____

   _____

   _____

   _____

   _____

   _____

   _____

   _____

   _____

   _____

   _____

   _____

Making Your Mark Plus: The Sum of Things

You now have a good description of your company and a sense of what is important to the company value system. You also have a double-tiered definition of your audience and the inside story on your audience's emotions.

Drawing on the profile information you've gathered, summarize your audience's agenda as follows for future reference:

- Your company's values _____

_____

_____

_____

_____

_____

- Your target audience—management and above _____

_____

_____

_____

_____

_____

- Your target audience—peers and support _____

_____

_____

_____

_____

_____

- "Emotion detector" highlights_____

_____

_____

_____

_____

_____

_____

- Other insights and information you've gained from this chapter

_____

_____

_____

_____

_____

_____

_____

Now you're ready to analyze the product—you!

3

Product Profile:

The Good News About You

- **The Cheerleader:** "Nobody has to ask Stacy twice what's new in her life. She volunteers the information."

- **The Powerhouse:** "I'm glad Bill's on our committee. Besides his reputation for being hard-working and honest, he's in great demand for brainstorming and problem-solving projects. Working with him is like working with a powerhouse."

- **Mr. Reliable:** "All I can say is Tom shows up on time, he does good work, he does extra when asked, and he never causes problems."

- **The Social Wonder:** "Susan knows everyone. Every time I go to the club, there she is, eating dinner with the CEO of a multinational corporation. I go to the symphony, she's there, too, hobnobbing with the mayor. Susan knows everyone."

- **The Problem-Solver Plus:** "Arthur knows how to get anything. You have a problem, you need something, call Arthur. He'll figure out how to help you."

- **The Inside Story:** "You want a grapevine gourmet—just talk to Lea. She has the scoop on everyone in the company and their families. And their dogs. For the inside story on what's really happening, call Lea."

- **All Work and No Play:** "I work hard, but Fred works harder. I leave at seven and he's still in his office. I dash in on Saturday morning and Fred's already here. He's always working."

- **The Information Ally:** "Aaron doesn't talk much, but when he does, I listen. That guy reads everything he can get his hands on. He's a fount of industry information."

- **Invisible Man/Woman:** "Who did you say? I'm sorry, I don't know Sally. What department did you say she's in?"

Imagine that each of these people is a product on a long corporate shelf. Each of them performs a different and valuable role in the company. Perhaps you're a combination of several. Notice the descriptive words for those "types" you feel closest to and apply them to yourself:

"I am (a) _____ ,

_____ ,

_____ , and

_____ ."

Now you're warmed up to find your selling power.

Negotiating Your Niche

Everyone—including you—has a unique style, a particular niche. An important step, therefore, in your self-marketing plan is defining the qualities you want to project. Think of yourself as a new product facing a competitive marketplace. Visualize yourself strolling through a grocery or hardware store, wheeling your basket past shelves brimming with choices. What makes you stop and select? Is it packaging, price, reputation, environmental impact, looks, quality, uniqueness?

Take a few moments now to complete "My Product Profile" on page 34. You can use these product-oriented marketing concepts as you begin to shape a strategic plan that addresses your company values and your audience needs.

My Product Profile

Packaging

1. Your packaging includes your dress, your image. Check off the following descriptions that apply:

   ☐ Premium-priced

   ☐ Budget edition

   ☐ Environmentally conscious

   ☐ Generic (you fit in anywhere)

   ☐ Gender specific (either particularly feminine or masculine)

   ☐ Economy size

   ☐ Other _____

2. Your packaging makes you:

   ☐ Stand out on the shelf

   ☐ Blend in

   ☐ Get lost in the display

3. Write a summary statement of your packaging style. ("Kate is premium-priced, environmentally conscious, and individualized. She stands out on the shelf."): _____

   _____

   _____

   _____

   _____

   _____

   _____

   _____

Making Your Mark

Placement on Shelf

1. Where do you fit in the company culture? Check off all descriptions that apply:

   ☐ Easy to find

   ☐ Easy to miss

   ☐ Too hard to reach

   ☐ Often gets shoved behind another product

   ☐ Understocked (unavailable)

   ☐ Overstocked (too available)

2. Write a one-sentence placement summary: _____

   _____

   _____

   _____

   _____

   _____

   _____

Perceived Value

Your value and your perceived value may have gaps. Check off your intuitive first response to the following questions:

1. How does your audience feel when they see you?

   ☐ Excited

   ☐ Indifferent

   ☐ Rushed

   ☐ Another person to deal with

   ☐ Another problem

   ☐ Other_____

2. How do they feel about investing (time, money) in you?

☐ You pay big dividends

☐ The interest rate is too low

☐ Your stock fluctuates too wildly

☐ No growth potential

☐ Great potential but random performance

3. What do they expect from you?

☐ Exactly what they ask for

☐ More than what they ask for

☐ Less than what they ask for

☐ Always a surprise

☐ Random performance

4. Write a summary about how your audience feels: _____

_____

_____

_____

_____

_____

5. How do you want them to feel? _____

_____

_____

_____

_____

_____

Shelf Space

The more shelf space you occupy, the more chance you have of
getting noticed.

1. What percentage of your potential audience do you currently
   know? _____

   _____

2. Do those you don't know have any particular motivation for
   getting to know you? _____

Going Far Along the Way

Now that you've looked closely at your current shelf appeal, the next step is to discover areas where you can boost your visibility. Analyze the Features, Added Benefits, and Results of what you currently do—discover your FAR-reaching appeal!

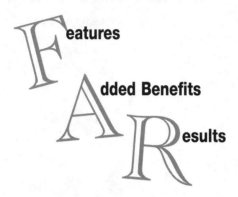

Features. Features translate into the physical actions or aspects of your job—word processing, project management, sales, marketing, and so forth. Be as specific as possible.

For example, Jocelyn is an executive assistant to the vice president. One of the features of her job is typing.

Added benefits. What added benefits do your features provide? That is, how does your work help people in the company? The benefits tap into the needs of your audience. Take your time exploring the ways people benefit from your work. Ask a couple of co-workers or friends for a quick brainstorming session on this topic.

When asked how she adds benefits to her company, Jocelyn says, "I help my company project a professional image through correspondence that's clear, concise, and correct. I also help employee relations by making sure the memos that leave our office are friendly in tone."

Results. What happens as a result of you doing your job? How does your work translate into action? Jocelyn says, "As a result of clear correspondence, my company has a good reputation with its clients. We seldom have complaints or disagreements because of unclear written communication. We seldom alienate our employees by sending out half-thought-through memos."

Take some time to create your own "FAR Chart" (see p.40). Work on this project for several days, so you can include all the things you do. The more you're able to divide your tasks into small "pieces," the more successful you'll be in adding to your pile of features and benefits.

But don't stop with your job. You also have a life outside of work—and that's worth looking at too. Make a list of your FAR-reaching effects in the community and home, including the organizations you belong to, the volunteer work you do, and your accomplishments outside the work arena.

FAR
FAR Chart:
Your Work

Features	Added Benefits	Results

FAR Chart:
Your Present Home/Community Involvement

Features	Added Benefits	Results

Checking Your Wattage

After all this analysis of your "product" self, step back and take a look at where you shine and where you barely flicker. What are your areas of exceptional strength? What areas can you enhance?

First, take five or six minutes to brainstorm the things you're really good at and the reasons people like you. Don't spend more than three minutes on each topic and don't be modest. Jot down anything that comes to mind. Recall any compliment you've received in the workplace. Save this list—it's worth having when you feel down and insecure.

Things I'm Really Good At

Next, brainstorm on the areas where you feel insecure. Take five minutes or so to jot down some fears (things you stay away from because you don't believe you have the expertise, people situations that make you uneasy, etc.).

Areas Where I Feel Insecure

_____

_____

_____

_____

_____

_____

_____

_____

_____

_____

_____

_____

_____

Now, gather input from a few mentors and people whose opinions you trust. Ask these people for feedback on your strong points and, if you're open for it, how you could improve.

44 Making Your Mark Plus: The Sum of Things

You've analyzed your product and drawn a complete map of where you are now. You've looked at your present and your potential. You've analyzed your work features, added benefits, and results, as well as your strengths and benefits at home and in the community.

Now write a summary of your strengths: _____

_____

_____

_____

_____

_____

_____

_____

Considering your company values and audience needs, what areas do you want to strengthen?

_____

_____

_____

_____

_____

_____

_____

Who can help you? _____

_____

_____

_____

_____

_____

_____

_____

What are the first three steps to take?

1. _____

2. _____

3. _____

Now you're ready for help. Don't do it all alone: Build a team of people for your marketing support.

4

Power Partners:

You Don't Have to Do This Alone

• When you think of sports, you think of George. Sure, he's a computer programmer by trade, but he always has a blurb on sports in the company newsletter. He's often quoted in the newspaper, and he usually has some sports trivia contest going. You don't care that much about sports, but with George around, you can't help but get interested.

- Evelyn, the assistant in public relations, is the unchallenged grammar queen. Although everyone has a dictionary, most people consult Evelyn—it's just plain friendlier to have her explain word usage than to struggle through the style manual. Sometimes Evelyn sends out grammar memos. She words things with such wit that it doesn't even feel like criticism.

- You have out-of-town company and want to impress them with a delicious, interesting meal, so you call Sandra in accounting. She not only eats out often, she's also a member of three gourmet clubs. Sandra's the last word on what's in and what's inedible.

These three are master marketers—you can probably think of similar people in your own company. You need to know who they are and what they want. That way, you can differentiate. It's not a question of competition, because there are enough needs to go around. It's a question of differentiation. You wouldn't move into a crowded apartment—why try to fill a niche that's already brimming with people?

Spotting Master Marketers As Potential Mentors

To identify master marketers, look around for people who:

- Everyone seems to know.

- Have an expertise in some area.

- Are often quoted in the newspaper or company newsletter.

- Serve on every committee.

Notice the areas where they are most prominent. Is their expertise computer software? Are they known for having a gourmet palate? Do they have the inside story on company trends? Do they know a joke for every occasion? How do their areas of visibility tie in with company values? with audience needs?

Once you have a list of names and visible specialties, notice people on the list who can best support you. Pay attention to these attributes:

- People in a different work area

- People with a different management style

- People with a different expertise

- People known to be team-oriented

- People you have an introduction to (if you're in a big company)

- People you'd like to talk and work with

- People with different strengths and interests

- People with status and their own following in the company

Armed with your list, select three people to approach, starting with the person who seems the best match for you. The purpose of your meeting is to:

- Learn more about this person's marketing success (Was it intentional or did it just naturally happen?).

- Learn from any mistakes this person made.

- Ask for advice on becoming more visible (What areas do they see a need to develop?).

- Ask what to expect when you become more visible (What are the negative aspects of visibility?).

- Ask how you can help each other (If you're an expert on etiquette and protocol, for example, maybe you could add a P.S. to one of Evelyn's memos, or since you're the king of barbecue, you could share the lowdown with Sandra.).

The right people add potential and potency to your marketing plan. Choosing the right mentor can make a big difference in your marketing success.

Your ideal mentor:

- Understands and is connected with your target audiences.
- Understands the company values.
- Values your areas of strength.
- Has connections that can help you become more visible.
- Is politically astute and has a solid reputation.
- Has a couple of hours a month to work with you on your marketing plan.
- Knows how to be an advocate and a cheerleader.

Once you find a mentor, make sure you hold up your end of the relationship. Protect your mentor's time. Learn from but don't take advantage of his or her expertise. Keep your meetings short and focused, and have an agenda each time that includes your new ideas, ready to implement; a progress report from the period since your last meeting; and your goals for the next month. Be prepared to make changes in your ideas and to take your mentor's advice.

If you can't find a company mentor, look outside your company:

"I've been searching for two years, and I still can't find a mentor in my company," Carol says. Carol works for a big company and wants a woman mentor to help her get more visible. However, so far there are no women in positions of visibility that she has easy access to.

Carol decided to approach Sally, an ad executive she'd met at her breakfast club. Sally agreed to be her mentor. Because Sally wasn't personally familiar with the company culture, Carol shared summaries of her audience's agenda (from Chapter 2) and Sally shared her expertise in advertising. Sally gave Carol fresh ideas that she could translate into her company system.

If you can't find a mentor, don't worry. There are plenty of other ways to get help. Most people love to share ideas. Give your co-workers and friends a chance to be part of your rising success. Invite them to a brainstorming lunch. Don't feel shy at being the center of attention at these Lunch Bunch gatherings. You'll gladly return the favor for them sometime.

Take the ideas you've formed (on your own or with your mentor) and share these with your lunch group. Ask what they like about each idea, what their reservations are about each idea, and how they could improve on the ideas.

Make a list of who else can help you, such as people in other departments, vendors, even clients. Ask your friends how they can help. Does one want to volunteer to be your encourager? Can you share your goals with your encourager and have that person check in on you once or twice a month? How else can your friends help you? How will your self-marketing be helpful to them?

Meet with your Lunch Bunch every month or so. If you meet more often, make it a mutual support group: Help the other members work on their goals too.

52   Making Your Mark Plus: The Sum of Things

Now you don't have to worry about being moody, having an attack of low self-esteem, feeling overwhelmed by your goals, thinking "I can't do this!" You have a support team to cheer you on. Make a list—this crew is vital. Keep it posted to boost your energy and remind you that you don't have to do it all.

Mentor

Name: _____

Address: _____

Phone: _____

Agreement _____

Lunch Bunch

Name: _____

Address: _____

Phone: _____

Name: _____

Address: _____

Phone: _____

Name: _____

Address: _____

Phone: _____

Name: _____

Address: _____

Phone: __ _____

Encourager

Name: _____

Address: _____

Phone: _____

Other People Who Will Help

Name: _____

Address: _____

Phone: _____

Name: _____

Address: _____

Phone: _____

Positioning Poses:

Creating the Perception

$\mathbb{T}$he magician calls Henry to the front of the room. "I heard your ears have been bothering you, Henry. I think I can help." He pulls two red balls from Henry's right ear.

"Your problem isn't solved yet," the magician says, and then pulls three red balls from Henry's left ear.

Sure, the audience knows there weren't really five foam balls stuffed into Henry's ears (although he was a little out of it in the last staff meeting...). The magician's confident demeanor and image created the perception that his magic was real. To prepare your audience to believe how great you are, you need to create the proper image, too, and then drum up the demand.

Telling your story is crucial to your marketing campaign. Decide on the image you want to project—competent? thoughtful? a real go-getter?—and then create your positioning prowess. Revisit your audience agenda summary sheet and your list of strengths. Look at the FAR Chart you filled out describing your present job.

Now get ready to "talk" to yourself.

Mirror, Mirror: Analyzing Your Image

Your image starts with YOU. Everything in your personal environment can support or detract from it.

So far, you've analyzed your current image, what your audience thought of you, and whether your audience knows you. You've analyzed company values and audience needs, and seen where the niches are filled and where the needs are unmet.

Now it's time to get a complete picture of your image and decide what you want to change and what is perfect exactly as it is. The exercise on page 57, "The Projection Screen," offers a nifty tool to help you do this. After completing it, analyze each category. What's good? What could be better? These are image reflectors that work for you even when you're not there. Use them as part of your support team.

The Projection Screen

Answer these questions for yourself, and then get feedback from friends and co-workers. Your self-image and their image of you may be different.

1. Your clothes are:

   ☐ Professional   ☐ Artistic

   ☐ Friendly   ☐ Eclectic

   ☐ Stylish   ☐ Ill-fitting

2. Your expression is typically:

   ☐ Smiling   ☐ Serious

   ☐ Thoughtful   ☐ Angry

   ☐ Quizzical   ☐ Distracted

3. Your speaking pattern is usually:

   ☐ Professional   ☐ Aloof

   ☐ Friendly   ☐ Inviting

   ☐ Awkward   ☐ Hesitant

4. Your body language says:

   ☐ Talk to me   ☐ Get out of my way

   ☐ I'm important   ☐ I'm quite busy, but stop me if you need to

5. Your desk says:

   ☐ I'm organized   ☐ I'm too busy for words

   ☐ You can count on me   ☐ Don't hand me another paper

6. Your office wall says:

   ☐ I'm smart   ☐ I'm educated

   ☐ I receive awards   ☐ I love my kids

   ☐ I love my work   ☐ I'm a team player

   ☐ I'm a deep thinker

7. Your office furniture says:

☐ Come in, let's talk   ☐ I mean business
☐ Don't stay too long   ☐ I'm important
☐ I welcome visitors

8. Listen to your voice mail message. What does it say?

_____

How is the tone? (warm, abrupt, etc.)

_____

Does it really invite people to call back?

☐ Yes   ☐ No

Do you leave enough time for a message?

☐ Yes   ☐ No

9. Does your business card reflect any of your personality or philosophy?

☐ Yes   ☐ No

Is there anything interesting or memorable on the card?

☐ Yes   ☐ No

10. Reread some of your internal communications—your memos and letters. The image you are projecting is:

☐ Personable   ☐ No-nonsense
☐ Information only   ☐ Playful
☐ Caring

Now that you've gathered information about your image, think about how you can enhance it to better reflect company values and audience needs. What is the ideal image for you to project? What are some simple ways you can spruce up this image? Review the completed "Projection Screen" and write down the following:

Things That Work With My Image

1. _____

2. _____

3. _____

4. _____

5. _____

Things I Want to Add or Change

1. I want to change_____

_____

   Who can help me? _____

   What steps do I take?_____

2. I want to change_____

_____

   Who can help me? _____

   What steps do I take?_____

3. I want to change_____

_____

   Who can help me? _____

   What steps do I take?_____

4. I want to change_____

_____

Who can help me? _____

What steps do I take?_____

Put your image to work for you while you work on other marketing angles.

6

Power Plan: Implementing

Your Marketing Strategies

- "I'd like to be CEO, but no woman has ever gone beyond manager in my company."

- "I'd love to move into the marketing department, but my writing skills aren't strong enough."

- "If only someone from corporate would notice me, I know I'd be promoted."

62

How often do scenes of success drift into your mind? You'd like more money, more prestige, more visibility, more recognition, more responsibility...

Whatever "more" motivates you, now is the time to push beyond wishful thinking and make it happen.

To get to what you really want, to make your marketing plan really work for you, send your imagination out beyond what you think is possible. Your thoughts should become bold, outrageous, invincible!

The WIDES thinking model broadens your way of approaching work through the following process:

ild thinking—Untame yourself and visualize what you really want.

ncorporate—Combine the elements of your vision into one focus statement.

elineate—Write down things you can do to make your vision come true, and make a list of specific short-term goals.

valuate—Analyze and prioritize your goals.

chedule—Put one goal a week on your calendar.

Here's a breakdown of how the WIDES method works:

1. **Wild thinking.** When you untame yourself, you can imagine the top, the apex, the bountiful best. Wild thinking helps you see the overall picture. It pushes your vision of yourself beyond a narrow niche and into a panorama of possibilities. Wild thinking prevents you from limiting your possibilities.

   When possible, practice wild thinking with friends or co-workers. This builds energy and gives you *all* permission to think big. Before you begin, review the rules of brainstorming:

   1. Defer judgment. Every idea is worthy of being noted.

   2. Choose a scribe to write down every idea, just the way the person says it (don't edit). If you're alone, simply scribble your ideas.

   3. Don't comment or ask questions during the process.

   4. Work quickly—the faster the ideas fly, the more creative you'll get. You're inviting your subconscious out.

   5. Set a time limit. For example, take five minutes and try to come up with twenty ideas. Then take another five minutes and double the amount of ideas. This timed pressure helps you let loose.

   Start out your wild thinking with a phrase such as "It would it be truly wonderful if my marketing plan worked so well that..." Say anything that comes to mind as quickly as you can; don't edit or judge yourself.

For example, "It would be truly wonderful if my marketing plan worked so well that...

- My boss noticed how great I was and nominated me for a Nobel Prize."

- The shareholders suggested I step in as CEO."

- I got a 200 percent raise."

- My peers treated me to a lavish dinner."

- Oprah invited me to be a guest on her show."

- A Hollywood agent called and wanted to create a film based on my work experience."

- The mayor of the city proclaimed a holiday in my honor."

"At first, I felt stupid saying these fanciful things," Candace said. "Then I started having fun, feeling the potential. At the end of five minutes, I felt like I could do anything."

2. **Incorporate.** Once you sense your power, incorporate all the elements of your wildness into one wishful statement: "It would be truly wonderful if my boss, the CEO, and the shareholders noticed how great I was and awarded me a huge raise, nominated me for a Nobel peace prize, and gave me time off to create a film based on my work experience."

(Is your mind already sliding back to reality? Perhaps you're thinking, "Yeah, if I were that great everybody would be really threatened by me and I'd probably be downsized, rightsized, or cut down to size." Ignore that nagging pessimism and stay in the wildlands.)

3. Delineate. Now combine your wish with your audience's needs and the company's values. Delineate the behaviors that will meet these needs and make your statement come to pass. Review your audience analysis and your FAR Chart. Look at putting together all the elements:

- What the audience wants

- Your strengths and the image you want to project

- Your features and benefits

You might ask yourself some questions: What would it take for my boss notice me? What would it take for the CEO and shareholders to think I was great? How can I meet my company's values of community service? How can I meet my audience's need to have more support?

Brainstorm, either alone or with a group, on ways to get noticed. Here are some examples to get you started:

- Contribute to an employee newsletter.

- Start an employee newsletter.

- Instigate fund-raising for a local charity.

- Begin a recycling campaign.

- Start a news-clipping service, sharing time management news or other information your audience might value.

- Start a cartoon of the week memo.

- Become an expert in some area that honors company values and meets your audience's emotional needs.

- Create a monthly accomplishment page for your supervisors that lists things you've done in the workplace and elsewhere.

- Design a poster that gives people fun and informative facts, and place it outside your office.

- Host a celebration for your department (for example, send out invitations to "Terrific Tuesday" and bring in doughnuts and apples to brighten a weekday morning).

- Volunteer for different committees at work (find out which ones give you the most visibility).

Make a big long list, and then combine statements to come up with at least ten ideas you like.

4. **Evaluate.** Evaluate your goals and prioritize them. For example, set some criteria, and then rank each goal numerically. Your criteria might include what takes the least amount of your time or money, or what offers you the most visibility.

Once you've chosen your primary goals, you can break them down into small steps. For example, if one goal is to contribute to the employee newsletter, your steps might include:

- Reading several issues of the newsletter to see what kinds of articles the employees enjoy.

- Calling the editor to find out the submission process (ask what types of articles are needed and what the deadlines are).

- Selecting a topic that puts you in contact with important people from other departments (such as an interview with a CFO).

- Finding a mentor to help you prepare for your interview and to review your article.

5. Schedule. It's not enough just to have goals; you must also schedule them. That is, put them in ink on your calendar. Make your goals bite-size (easy to do in a short period of time) and schedule them as though they are as concrete and as vital as the Wednesday morning department meeting. They are.

Your goals are your key to greater visibility and responsibility at work. To help you work through this strategic process, turn to the "WIDES Worksheet" on page 69.

1. Wild thinking. Jot down some wishful thinking and dreaming.

_____

_____

_____

_____

_____

_____

2. Incorporate. Write down your focus statement.

_____

_____

_____

_____

3. Delineate. Make a list of specific short-term goals. Use your FAR Chart to extend things you are already doing. How can you capitalize on work you're already involved in?

_____

_____

_____

_____

_____

4. Evaluate. Select criteria and prioritize your goals.

My criteria are:

_____

_____

_____

_____

My prioritized goals are:

_____

_____

_____

_____

Now break your goals down into small steps.

My steps for Goal #1 are:

_____

_____

_____

_____

5. Schedule. Place one goal (step) a week on your calendar, on the date you intend to do it.

Goal   Date

January 20

You've reached for the ceiling and beyond. You've developed a vision for yourself. Now all you have to do is make it happen.

Use the tools you've created. Rely on your support group. Dare to dream and reach out to be the most visible, valuable, and sought-after employee you can be.

Following Through: Making Your Plan

Work Over the Long Haul

The more visible you are, the more valuable you are. Try your self-marketing plan for six to twelve months and see how it's working. Are you reaching the most people with the least amount of work? Is the image you're projecting still right for your company? Have you added any interests or duties that can benefit you and your company?

Do a quick update periodically of your FAR Charts as well as your strengths and challenges.

74

Revise your audience analysis summaries as needed. Then revisit your WIDES Worksheet and target yourself for even more success.

Your industry is changing. Are those changes predictable? Will they affect you and your performance? Will they change the way your company looks at things? Try to imagine what your company will be like in five years. See yourself and your role in the company. What will be the needs of your audience? What changes in services, distribution, clients do you foresee?

You may be guessing or using your intuition on some of these answers. But even if the information is not totally accurate, it helps you to have it written down.

The point is, you must constantly update your plan in order to make it work for you. Anticipating changes can help you do this. You must also be prepared to adapt your plan to circumstances you didn't expect.

Having a written marketing plan will give you a foundation for making yourself more visible—beginning NOW. Developing an active mindset will help you keep your plan flexible so it will continue to serve you in the future.

Bibliography &

Suggested Reading

Caroselli, Marlene, and David Harris. *Risk-Taking: 50 Ways to Turn Risks Into Rewards*. Mission, KS: SkillPath Publications, 1993.

Clarke, Colleen. *Networking: How to Creatively Tap Your People Resources*. Mission, KS: SkillPath Publications, 1993.

Dudley, Denise. *Every Woman's Guide to Career Success*. Mission, KS: SkillPath Publications, 1991.

Feder, Michal E. *Taking Charge: A Personal Guide to Managing Projects and Priorities*. Mission, KS: SkillPath Publications, 1993.

Friedman, Paul. *How to Deal With Difficult People (revised)*. Mission, KS: SkillPath Publications, 1991.

Mallory, Charles. *Publicity Power: A Practical Guide to Effective Promotion*. Los Altos, CA: Crisp Publications, 1989.

Morgan, Rebecca L. *Professional Selling: Practical Secrets for Successful Sales*. Los Altos, CA: Crisp Publications, 1988.

Poley, Michelle Fairfield. *A Winning Attitude: How to Develop Your Most Important Asset*. Mission, KS: SkillPath Publications, 1992.

Shouse, Deborah. *Breaking the Ice: How to Improve Your On-the-Spot Communication Skills*. Mission, KS: SkillPath Publications, 1994.

Siress, Ruth Herrman, Carolyn Riddle, and Deborah Shouse. *Working Woman's Communications Survival Guide*. Englewood Cliffs, NJ: Prentice Hall, 1994.

Withers, Jean, and Carol Vipperman. *Marketing Your Service: A Planning Guide for Small Businesses*. Seattle: Self-Counsel Press, 1987.

Available From SkillPath Publications

Self-Study Sourcebooks

Climbing the Corporate Ladder: What You Need to Know and Do to Be a Promotable Person *by Barbara Pachter and Marjorie Brody*

Coping With Supervisory Nightmares: 12 Common Nightmares of Leadership and What You Can Do About Them *by Michael and Deborah Singer Dobson*

Defeating Procrastination: 52 Fail-Safe Tips for Keeping Time on Your Side *by Marlene Caroselli, Ed.D.*

Discovering Your Purpose *by Ivy Haley*

Going for the Gold: Winning the Gold Medal for Financial Independence *by Lesley D. Bissett, CFP*

Having Something to Say When You Have to Say Something: The Art of Organizing Your Presentation *by Randy Horn*

Info-Flood: How to Swim in a Sea of Information Without Going Under *by Marlene Caroselli, Ed.D.*

The Innovative Secretary *by Marlene Caroselli, Ed.D.*

Letters & Memos: Just Like That! *by Dave Davies*

Mastering the Art of Communication: Your Keys to Developing a More Effective Personal Style *by Michelle Fairfield Poley*

Organized for Success! 95 Tips for Taking Control of Your Time, Your Space, and Your Life *by Nanci McGraw*

A Passion to Lead! How to Develop Your Natural Leadership Ability *by Michael Plumstead*

P.E.R.S.U.A.D.E.: Communication Strategies That Move People to Action *by Marlene Caroselli, Ed.D.*

Productivity Power: 250 Great Ideas for Being More Productive *by Jim Temme*

Promoting Yourself: 50 Ways to Increase Your Prestige, Power, and Paycheck *by Marlene Caroselli, Ed.D.*

Proof Positive: How to Find Errors Before They Embarrass You *by Karen L. Anderson*

Risk-Taking: 50 Ways to Turn Risks Into Rewards *by Marlene Caroselli, Ed.D. and David Harris*

Speak Up and Stand Out: How to Make Effective Presentations *by Nanci McGraw*

Stress Control: How You Can Find Relief From Life's Daily Stress *by Steve Bell*

The Technical Writer's Guide *by Robert McGraw*

Total Quality Customer Service: How to Make It Your Way of Life *by Jim Temme*

Write It Right! A Guide for Clear and Correct Writing *by Richard Andersen and Helene Hinis*

Your Total Communication Image *by Janet Signe Olson, Ph.D.*

Handbooks

The ABC's of Empowered Teams: Building Blocks for Success *by Mark Towers*

Assert Yourself! Developing Power-Packed Communication Skills to Make Your Points Clearly, Confidently, and Persuasively *by Lisa Contini*

Breaking the Ice: How to Improve Your On-the-Spot Communication Skills
by Deborah Shouse

The Care and Keeping of Customers: A Treasury of Facts, Tips, and Proven Techniques for Keeping Your Customers Coming BACK! *by Roy Lantz*

Challenging Change: Five Steps for Dealing With Change *by Holly DeForest and Mary Steinberg*

Dynamic Delegation: A Manager's Guide for Active Empowerment *by Mark Towers*

Every Woman's Guide to Career Success *by Denise M. Dudley*

Grammar? No Problem! *by Dave Davies*

Great Openings and Closings: 28 Ways to Launch and Land Your Presentations With Punch, Power, and Pizazz *by Mari Pat Varga*

Hiring and Firing: What Every Manager Needs to Know *by Marlene Caroselli, Ed.D. with Laura Wyeth, Ms.Ed.*

How to Be a More Effective Group Communicator: Finding Your Role and Boosting Your Confidence in Group Situations *by Deborah Shouse*

How to Deal With Difficult People *by Paul Friedman*

Learning to Laugh at Work: The Power of Humor in the Workplace
by Robert McGraw

Making Your Mark: How to Develop a Personal Marketing Plan for Becoming More Visible and More Appreciated at Work *by Deborah Shouse*

Meetings That Work *by Marlene Caroselli, Ed.D.*

The Mentoring Advantage: How to Help Your Career Soar to New Heights
by Pam Grout

Minding Your Business Manners: Etiquette Tips for Presenting Yourself Professionally in Every Business Situation *by Marjorie Brody and Barbara Pachter*

Misspeller's Guide *by Joel and Ruth Schroeder*

Motivation in the Workplace: How to Motivate Workers to Peak Performance and Productivity *by Barbara Fielder*

NameTags Plus: Games You Can Play When People Don't Know What to Say
by Deborah Shouse

Networking: How to Creatively Tap Your People Resources *by Colleen Clarke*

New & Improved! 25 Ways to Be More Creative and More Effective *by Pam Grout*

Power Write! A Practical Guide to Words That Work *by Helene Hinis*

The Power of Positivity: Eighty ways to energize your life *by Joel and Ruth Schroeder*

Putting Anger to Work For You *by Ruth and Joel Schroeder*

Reinventing Your Self: 28 Strategies for Coping With Change *by Mark Towers*

Saying "No" to Negativity: How to Manage Negativity in Yourself, Your Boss, and Your Co-Workers *by Zoie Kaye*

The Supervisor's Guide: The Everyday Guide to Coordinating People and Tasks
by Jerry Brown and Denise Dudley, Ph.D.

Taking Charge: A Personal Guide to Managing Projects and Priorities
by Michal E. Feder

Treasure Hunt: 10 Stepping Stones to a New and More Confident You! *by Pam Grout*

A Winning Attitude: How to Develop Your Most Important Asset!
by Michelle Fairfield Poley

For more information, call 1-800-873-7545.